Horst To Holyoke

Horst To Holyoke

A Father-Daughter Memoir about Storytelling,
Memory, and Meaning Making.

Nicole Shea

FOE
Publishing
BALTIMORE

In memory of my father

Horst Ollmann

1935 – 20___

A good teacher is one who helps you become who you feel yourself to be. A good teacher is also one who says something that you won't understand until ten years later.

Julius Lester
1939 – 2018

Contents

What is a *Horst*?

Horst is the German word for a large nest.

Nest is nest. In English and in German.

A *Horst* specifically refers to a LARGE nest,
the kind a stork makes.

Where is Horst?

Horst was a place, years ago. It no longer exists but you can find it on maps today as Niechorze, Poland.

Horst Seebad was a small seaside resort in the State of Pomerania on the Baltic Sea.

The story is told that German sailors thought the coastline resembled a large nest. And so it was named, Horst, the word for a large nest in their language.

Who is Horst?

My grandparents on my father's side are Paul and Gertrude Ollmann. Paul was a barber-beautician by trade. Gertrude primarily worked taking care of the home and family. She also helped in the beauty and barber shop, and later cleaned and cooked for Russian soldiers. Paul called his wife Trudie or Trudchen – *chen*, a German suffix used as an endearment. Their first child was born on January 19th, 1930, a daughter named Charlotte. Charlotte would be the only girl to help her mother with the five brothers that followed: Heinz in 1931; Horst in 1935; Wilhelm in 1938; Rudolf in 1942; and the youngest, Johannes, who was born after the war.

This is a story by and about Horst Ollmann, my father.

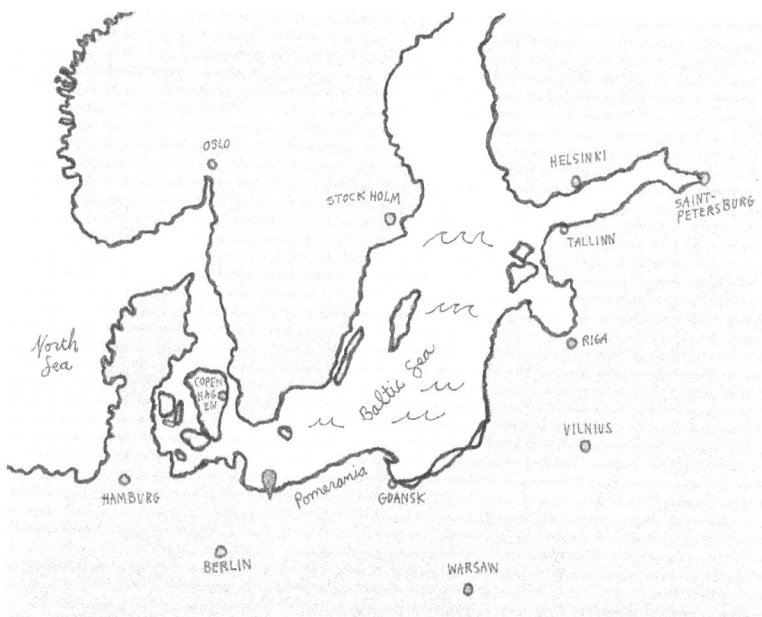

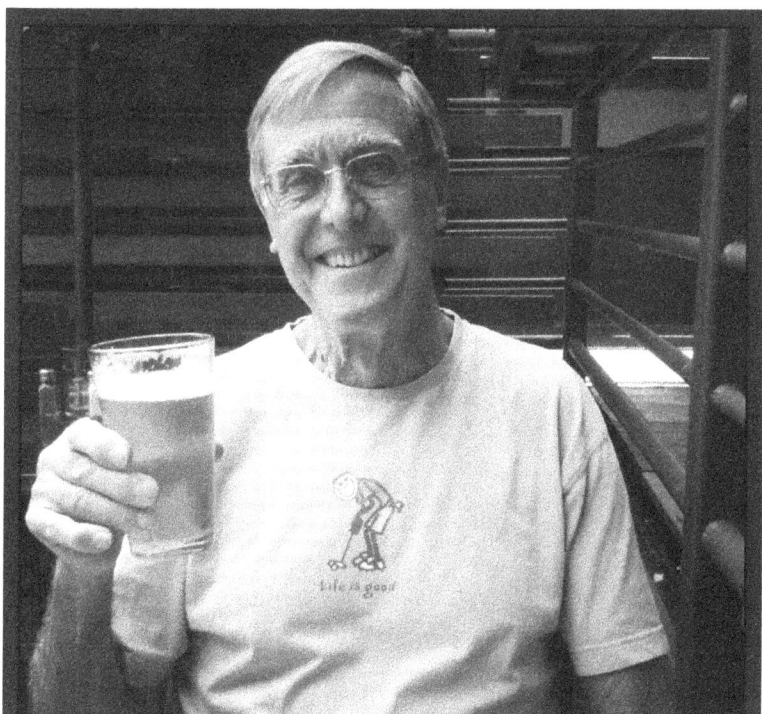

3

Author's Note

In 2016 my father proposed that I write a book about his childhood experiences during WWII. He'd read my zine *Shot In The Head* and liked the way I put the story together. I suggested that he record the stories he wanted to be included in the book. Horst was 81 years old when he curated these recollections for your enjoyment. I transcribed the recordings and conducted a follow-up interview. I tried to remain as true to the recordings as possible. If you know Horst, I hope you can hear him in his stories. If you do not, I recommend reading in your mind with an enthusiastic, sing-songy, German accent.

Over the past six years, we have discussed storytelling, our history, and what this project would become. Working on the book, we were able to revisit the events and experiences that shaped who we became. That led to the book's second half, my stories about being Horst's daughter.

Before we started this project, I'd already noticed ways in which my father was changing. I thought I understood the reason behind his question, "How long will it take to write this book?" It was my first question too. I chose six years based on a book recommendation I read in preparation. It was also an unspoken hope that my father would somehow stubbornly live long enough to see its completion. We remain stubbornly determined and still kicking.

Part I: HORST

Leichenblässe

That I am still alive I can only credit one lady. She came to my dad's barber and beauty shop where my mom was working at the same time and she wanted to see my mom's new boy, me. My mom said, 'No, I can't right now, I'm busy, but my dad said, Gertrude, *go*.' It was a short walk to the house where I was in the living room in a baby carriage, to stay warm. My dad's barber and beauty shop was on my grandmother Oma Wilke's property. When they opened the door to the living room it was full of smoke. What had happened was one of the briquets from the tile oven had fallen against the door and snapped the lid open and landed on the wooden floor. The wooden floor started to burn, smolder, it never really got flames, but it just filled the room with a lot of smoke. So my mom took me outside in the carriage, and right away they called the doctor. The doctor said there isn't much we can do, he already has the *Leichenblässe*, the color of a dead person, white, pale. The doctor said to keep me outside and cover me with blankets to keep me warm and maybe I will come around. Little by little I recovered. Well, I'll tell you what, that had repercussions many years later.

9

Warmth

The lake between the town of Horst and Eiersberg was called Eiersberger See. There was a heavy reed growing there and that was cut down for roofing in that part of the country. You saw a lot of homes covered with the reed, about twelve inches thick, warm, and no rain ever got through. It was a wonderful thing. My grandmother's house was like that. That was good for us when we had bows and arrows. I was tall enough to reach the edge and pull a straw out. Put something in front with a nail, then we could go duck hunting.

Oma Wilke was not really my relation, but we always called her that and she was always there for us. She was important. In the wintertime when I went to see my grandmother, she had a bench in front of the *Kachelofen* and it was always so nice and cozy there. And then she would make me a sandwich. My uncle hunted ducks. They smoked those ducks and then they would cut slices off it and put it on a sandwich. It was good! More than once I had been at that *Kachelofen* and ate those sandwiches.

Cooling

In those days we did not have refrigerators. So, the hotels in my hometown, in Horst, they came to the lake and drilled a hole through the ice. I think they had a handmade drill. That would cut through it eventually and break through the ice, ice might have been about twelve inches or thicker. Then they would use a saw with big teeth, stick it in the hole and keep cutting away. They cut out blocks that were then picked up by the hotel. They put it in the basement of the hotel covered with moss or some kind of insulant that would keep the ice cold. That's where they stored the beer and all the other drinkable items like wine. It was pretty interesting. That caught our attention. We had two big hotels, Centrale Hotel and one right back up by the Baltic, right off the dunes. I forget the name for that particular place, but they all came and picked up the ice.

Smoking Eel

My Onkel Hans used to fish on the Eiersberger See, on the lake. He caught eel, a lot of eel. The eel is a fish almost like catfish, they like to be on the bottom, and that water is dark, I wouldn't say muddy, but definitely not as clear as near the top. So the eel also took on that color, they were kind of dark. And to sell the

11

fish, as my Onkel always did, when he had enough of them, he would take them to the city called Trebto, not that far from my hometown Horst. But what happened is, when he caught the eel, he put them into a box with holes in it and put them near the shoreline on the Eiersberger See. And after a while, believe it or not, the fish took on a different color. They cleaned up and looked more like an eel that I remember. Then they were brought to the smokehouse. They would put a rod through the gills and hang one right next to the other, a whole bunch of them, in the smokehouse. Now, when all the fish were hanging in there, about two feet above the fire pit, first they would put in wood chips, that would more glow and bring the heat and that would actually cook the fish. Then when that was done, my Onkel and other people who did this, they could determine whether the fish was cooked. So then came the smoking. They put some stuff on top that was like I wouldn't say pine needles but something similar to it. That would create a lot of smoke. And you saw the smoke coming out of the cracks in the top. To keep the smoke in they would put wet sacks, like potato sacks, on top of that, so the smoke would stay in the chamber. The chamber, guessing, would be 4 by 6 feet, 4 feet wide 6 feet deep. They also knew how long it would take to smoke the fish. I think smoking was important because it would preserve the fish, the eel. Then they would take them out, and my Onkel Hans—he was a single man and that's all he ever did, catch fish, smoke 'em, and sell 'em—he put them in very thin wooden boxes, side by side, put a lid on it, then he would take them to the city of Trebto. That's where they would be sold on the market. That was my Onkel's job.

Vallgraben Ditch

As wintertime lost its grip on the country, on the air, on the ice, the meadows filled with water. The melting ice from the Eiersberger went into the brook that ran through the cow pastures. The brook was called Vallgraben, *Graben* is a ditch. It was fun for us because it flooded then it turned to ice, and it flooded again, so on top of the ice was water. What a fun time we had in our little sleds and ice picks to scoot around there and spray that water at each other. I call them ice picks, a stick with nails. Then one time we noticed the Vallgraben, since the water had receded, the ice had become like a roof. So I said to my friend Udo, 'You know, if we go real fast, at the brook, we might just scoot over it.' 'Yeah, we can do that,' he said. Of course, I would be the first one. Guess what happened? I hit that ice and went into the brook. I was up to my neck in the cold water! So now I gotta crawl outta there, which wasn't easy. What do you hang onto to pull yourself out? What I actually did was I found a little crack in the ice. I pulled myself up and my friend Udo said, 'You better get home to your mom, you're totally wet, it's cold, you gotta get home.' I said, 'No-no-no-no, I'm not gonna go to my mom, she's going to beat me up, I will go to my grandmother, Oma Wilke,' so that's where I went. She had a dry set of clothing for me, and I sat by the tile oven, and it felt so good and warm. The tile oven is called a *Kachelofen* and it is used for many things. To heat the room for one and my grandmother hung my wet clothes up there to dry. Also, another good thing, my grandmother had apple trees in the back. And in the winter, she put apples into a chamber in the oven where they would be roasted from the heat below. Eventually, when I got

13

home my mother never knew I fell into the Vallgraben. If I would have told my dad he would have laughed and said, 'Yeah, that sounds like you.'

Swallows

When the ice was gone the swallows would come back. When they came back, we knew it was summer. We always used to say, when you saw one, one swallow doesn't mean it is summer. So there had to be more, and there were, eventually. You know what they used to do, the swallows? On *Strand Strasse*, where my dad's barber shop was, they would come from the beach and very low. They would fly over the ground and we would try to stop them, to get in their way. Never managed it. They would get around us so quick, even two or three guys blocking the way, we could not stop them. They were amazing. So that was the start of summer.

Blueberry Picking

One thing my dad and I would do is go out and pick blueberries. What a tedious job that was. My dad let me use his bike and he borrowed another guy's bike. So we went into the woods, deep into the woods, where the blueberries were growing. First, we picked them by hand. That took forever to fill a bucket. Blueberries then weren't as big as I found out many years later in Massachusetts. These were like a quarter of the size of a cherry, very small. But what my dad found out—there is a tool you can use. It was like a shovel with teeth in the front. We used the tool through the branches and the leaves and picked out the blueberries. It

14

was messy because there were a lot of leaves mixed in with the blueberries. But my dad said, 'Don't worry about it. When the bucket is full, we get it all home and then we put it in a bucket of water and the leaves will float to the top and we skim them off and then we have the blueberries.' So we had blueberry jams my mother made. It was a good, good time!

Raspberry Picking

One important day I remember my dad took us out in the woods to pick raspberries. It was my sister Charlotte, myself, and my dad. We all had a little container to fill with raspberries. We had a bucket sitting nearby. When our little container was full of raspberries we went to the bucket, dumped it, and picked more. So, one time my sister Charlotte said, 'Horst, you fill your little container yet?' 'No-no, not yet, almost.' She said, 'From now on I want you to whistle because I think you are eating too many of them.' 'Ok,' so I whistled and picked the raspberries, and she was right, I filled the little container faster. When the bucket was full, we took it home, and then my mom got into action. She squeezed them until all the juice came out. I think she put them into a fine mesh or burlap bag, packed it real tight, and kept squeezing it. Then the juice was bottled. In the wintertime, we would have some kind of pudding and then put the raspberry juice on top of it. Kind of good memories, don't you think? I think it was good. I thought it was good then and I still think it was good!

Swimming

At age six-seven, I couldn't really swim. So we went into the water, two or three friends of mine, Udo that time, and two or three others. We were in maybe three-four feet of water. We had one foot on the ground and one up, so pretending we could swim. We did that for a while, but you know it didn't take long before we managed to float and swim. Came easy, but at first it wasn't because you never trusted the buoyancy. Freshwater and saltwater—big difference. Saltwater carries more than freshwater. So we managed eventually to swim. Then there were these places, we called them sandbanks. That's where the sand got piled up maybe about 50 yards out into the Baltic. When you could get there, you could stand again. That was exciting. There was sandbank number one and sandbank number two. I never made it to sandbank number two. That was a little bit further away. But I heard from bigger guys, like my brother Heinz, that you can stand there. 'I've done it,' he said, but I wasn't interested in doing that.

Homemade Kayaks

You know what else we did? We went to the Eiersberger and cut some heavy reeds. We cut them up, folded them, tied it all together, and made a kayak. And would you believe, it carried one person. You put it in the water, sat in it, and little by little push yourself off with your hands. And there I was, floating on the Baltic! That was an accomplishment because other kids would envy you for having done that, but they quickly learned how to do it. Then we had a whole bunch of people going out there in our little homemade kayaks.

On the Lake

I remember when my Onkel Hans came by and saw me on the lake. He couldn't believe what I was doing out there. I was sitting in a cover from a piece of furniture, the cover or lid of a furniture box. I don't know if I stole it or maybe it was already left behind by the Germans who escaped Pomerania, so it could have been that it belonged to nobody anymore. Most people by that time were gone, escaped to the west, not to get caught by the Russians. So what happened is, I got into this lid. It wasn't more than 5-6 inches deep, 6 inches at best. I slowly paddled out onto the lake. Then my Onkel comes by, 'What are you doing out there? You better get in here! Right now!' I said, 'Yes Onkel, yes Onkel Hans, Ich komme, I'm coming.' He couldn't see what I was sitting on. It was maybe a quarter of an inch above the water, the edge of the chest. If I would have made a lot of movements, I would have capsized. I don't know, by then I could probably swim, but it doesn't matter all that much, I wanted to get back *dry*. So slowly, with my hands, not to make any waves, I got back to the shore. I told my mom and dad, and my dad was pretty excited about what I did. He always liked when I did something crazy. There were plenty of chances for me to act crazy and I did all that.

Running

It was interesting for me to think back of that time because all summer long we ran around barefoot, into the fall. We went to school barefoot. My friend and I would meet on the *Clostergasse*, that was a little alleyway next to my grandmother Oma Wilke's house. We ran and then we got to an area where there was no sunshine on the ground, we kept running until we found a spot that was warmed up by the sun. There we waited until our feet got warm again. And we went from one sunny spot to another to finally get to school. School was interesting. It was on the outskirts of Horst going west. And I didn't like church all that, er, school, all that much, but we had to go, like everybody else. There we had one sports event and I got into a soccer game with the bigger boys. And teacher Huhlmann saw me running with a ball or chasing after guys who had the ball to take it away from them. He commented to my older brother, 'Heinz, your little brother, he can really run.'

Skating

I remember Christmas 1941. My dad always set up the Christmas tree in our barbershop because we really didn't have a large enough space in our apartment. But you know what I remember most, my dad got together with my godfather and they gave me a pair of skates. You attached the skates to your regular shoes, or boots if you had them, with a little key. I wasn't so good at first, but I loved going on to the big lake Eiersberger See. I forget how big it was, but it took my dad a half hour to walk across, on ice of course! So my dad, he would put me on his back with the skates on my feet, on my shoes, and I would go skating. I was on the ice all morning. Then he would come to the lake at lunch and whistle. He would carry me on his back to go home and there he put me in a chair. Under the table, I had the skates still on my feet. We would eat something and then he carried me back out to the ice and I skated all afternoon. That was crazy. At night when I went to bed, I still felt like I was skating.

Hockey

One thing we kids loved to do, if we were stable on our skates, was play hockey. A bunch of us would get together and we would find a spot away from the reeds, an open area, and there the ice was like a mirror. It was wonderful to skate and play hockey. These five guys against another five guys, or ten guys, we slammed these rocks around and had a great, great time playing against one another! Hockey sticks, you couldn't buy 'em. So we went into the woods and cut out a branch for each of us that looked like a hockey stick. It was just a wonderful time beating each other up!

Big Snow

It is January 1942 in my hometown Horst, in Pomerania, the state of Pomerania. Now what is so remarkable about that particular month is a huge snowstorm. According to my dad, there has never been that much snow in that town, in my hometown. The wind drift reached up to the rain gutter of my father's beauty and barber shop. The snow brings out all the kids. My friend Udo and his little brother Arno—they were the kids of the farmer Miller—they came over and we were romping around in the snow having a wonderful time.

Sleigh Bells

We had a lot of other good times. When there was some snow on the ground the farmers would come from Gross Horst with their horse-drawn sleighs and come through the town. When we heard the little sleigh bells, we hooked up our line from our sled and we were pulled along. Sometimes the—we call it coucher—that was controlling the horses, he used his whip and was trying to get us to get off it. But we stuck with it and so they pulled us through the whole town. Eventually, we got so far we said, you know, we gotta stop, we got a long way to walk back in the snow. So we let go of the line and dropped back and the coucher took off with his sleigh and we got back home.

Ice Floats

That was pretty much the end of memorable winter except for one thing. The Baltic was not as salty as the Atlantic or the North Sea, so we went on the ice floats playing catch. You jumped on one of them and then if it was big enough, it would carry you. That's what you always hoped for. But to get off it, to another big one, wasn't always guaranteed. So you get on another one, it held, you are lucky enough. Now, there were no big ones around anymore, and going back was not good because my friend was waiting to catch me. I jumped on a smaller one and guess what,

I went into the cold water of the Baltic, up to my waist. I walked to the shore and this time I had to go home. I went home and my mom was ok with it. I was surprised because she had so much work to do, she didn't have much patience for that kind of stuff. My dad was more understanding. Dry clothes on and we were fine again.

Igloo Hiding Spot

What also was a lot of fun was when the ice was coming in and the waves would break over the dunes. Dunes are two rows of pilings with big rocks in between. They were meant to break the waves so the waves wouldn't destroy the shoreline. When that piled up on the end of the dune, the ice piles were as big as this room. What we did first, everybody had some kind of tool, like a hatchet, we chopped into it from the end until it was big enough to get in, then we made it bigger yet. It was big enough for two people to sit in it! It was so much fun! That was our hiding spot! It was just wonderful memories. Believe me, it was special. And I remember one thing that also made the Baltic in winter special. My dad, many years before I was born, I think, he went on the ice, way out. There was a picture of him standing on an iceberg. It wasn't an iceberg that we're familiar with, it was piled up floats of ice. He was standing on top of it and he had a stick to balance himself around. That's the last thing I remember of winter in Horst Seebad.

Knife Trick

My brother Heinz, he had a bunch of friends older than me. They would go out together, playing together, doing things together, and I was too young for that group. So what happened, happened twice, once I had no inkling. They told me they needed a knife, 'Go into Oma Wilke and get a knife, we'll wait for you.' I come outside with my knife in my hand; there was nobody there. Ah ha, they were slick, they tried to get rid of me. They did it one more time, maybe a week, two weeks later. 'Horst, go and get a knife.' I said, 'No-no-no-no, you'll run away again.' I did not go inside, but you know, they let me go with them and they accepted me. I was probably faster than some of these other bigger kids. I was faster than my brother Heinz. I was not really a good brother to him because I teased him, and he went after me, and I stayed just far enough ahead of him that he couldn't catch me. Couldn't touch me. And he got so pissed. He was not happy that I outran him and he couldn't catch me. He couldn't tell his friends because they would never believe that I could outrun my older brother, but I did.

Cliff Push

Like I said, I wasn't really a good brother. I got to be a little older, maybe 7-8 years old and my dad was working in the German air force, maybe half an hour walk from my hometown. He was on a flight observation deck. He had to observe all flights, planes that flew through that area. He had to identify it, report the direction, and of course, what type of aircraft it was, usually small ones.

Then he had to report it to headquarters. One day, among many, Heinz and I had to bring food to my dad. My mom had this basket with lunch we had to carry up. Heinz carried it and we walked along the steep cliff towards the flight observation deck. Heinz was a nut about navigation, ships, boats, anything nautical. So he stopped, put the basket down, and looked at the sea. I said, 'Heinz, my friends are waiting for me in town, let's drop this off at dad's place and then I can go back.' 'Yeah-yeah-yeah-yeah,'

he said. He walked on again with the basket, maybe a hundred yards, and he stopped again and put the basket down. This time I had it. I gave him a shove and he went down off the edge, on his belly, running, sliding, and he landed right next to a big stone, a boulder maybe 10 feet in diameter. You know what the best sight was for me? When he got out of the sand and looked up at me and shook his fist. He said, 'I'm gonna get you, you wait when you come home.' So, I took the basket and brought it up to my dad. My dad said, 'Come on, stay a while.' And I said, 'No-no-no-no, I gotta go home, I gotta go home real bad.' I went home to Oma Wilke's house, and you know who was waiting for me, my brother Heinz. He looked like he was full of mud, which he was because he slid on his belly for quite a while, and this was like clay. So he came after me. My Oma Wilke took me behind her and said, 'You leave the boy alone because he's not done anything to you.' And Heinz said, 'Yes he has, look at me, I'm full of mud, he pushed me down the cliff!' 'Leave him alone.' Heinz took off and later he went to the barber shop and told my dad the story. My dad always came outside and whistled. So I went up there and said, 'What happened, what's the matter?' 'Heinz told me you pushed him off the cliff, look at him.' I said, 'Yup, I did because he always put the basket down and was looking at the ships and I wanted to get back to my friends in town.' 'But you shouldn't have kicked him off the cliff.' 'Yeah, maybe I shouldn't have.' So my dad said to Heinz, 'Heinz, if you ever come to me again complaining about your little brother, what he has done to you, you are going to get a kick in the butt from me.' Tell you what, that was the best lesson my brother could have learned. And I learned something too. Never to mess with Heinz because he would get me eventually.

Gold Pheasant

Across the street from where we lived was a railway station. And the man who ran the railway station also raised chickens. And I saw a chicken in front of a white rooster in front of the railway station, so I chased after it, to see if I could catch it. And it ran and ran and ran, around in circles, away from me, up and down, left and right. In those days they didn't have flush toilets, they had toilets where you go and do your business and you sit on a board with a hole in it and the bottom would be full of kaka. Anyhow, that white rooster went behind the wall and there were three toilets all with doors and the doors were open. And this rooster went into the last open door and I was right after it. The rooster flew up in the air and came back down, right through the hole, into the kaka. So the railway station manager found the rooster, went to my dad in the barbershop and complained about what I have done. My dad said, he was good at this, my dad said, 'Well, you had a white rooster, now you've got a gold pheasant.' I thought forever that was so funny. But my dad never reprimanded me, not about that. He wanted me to be active. Believe me, I was.

Opa and the Nazis

Did I mention when my dad walked into the hotel to play *Skat* and the Nazis were sitting there? Once a week my dad met two or three other guys and they played *Skat*, a card game. He walked into the hotel and three Nazis were sitting there with the swastika on their sleeve and instead of saying, like everybody was supposed to, Heil Hitler, he said, 'Heil Moscow.' That cost him. They smashed up the barber and beauty shop, mirrors, everything, hair dye against the wall, it was a mess. That's when my mom said to my dad, 'Paul, don't you think you should keep your mouth shut?' He said, 'yeah, I think I have to.'

The Russians March into My Hometown

The Russians march into my hometown around my 10th birthday. I'll never forget it. My mom and I were sitting at their bedroom window, and we looked onto the street and an ambulance came by. The door opened; blood ran out. The dead people they found, they picked them up, to identify or whatever was the reason I don't really know. They closed the door and off they went again. It wasn't a day later the Russians marched in. You know, they didn't have much to eat either. They came into the house looking for food which we didn't always have. We didn't have much to eat. I don't know how we got by; I don't really know. My mom was amazing, how she made something out of nothing. She always fed us, always put food on the table. It wasn't always so delicious, but it was food, and we knew if we don't eat it, there was nothing else. Eat it. And eating it we did.

Carved Snake

Around this time a Russian soldier came up to me. He had a raggedy military uniform. You could see he was in combat, not dressed for a parade. He showed me a snake he had whittled with a pocket knife out of a branch of a tree. He had cut sections about ⅝ of an inch and beveled all 4 sides to a 45-degree angle, so he could wiggle it. I thought he wanted money. I didn't know, I was just a kid. I rubbed my index finger and thumb together, the universal sign for money. He shook his head and pointed to his mouth and acted like he was chewing. I went into the house to show my mother the snake he had manufactured with his pocket knife. We had a little something to give, so my mom made him a sandwich and I brought it to him. He gobbled it down and then said, 'spasibo, spasibo,' in Russian it means thank you.

Sandwiches

Now the Russians were in town. And the part that was Gross Horst, the farmer's section, they hired German people. My mom was hired there to clean and cook, and she did, almost every day. They would beat her and kick her. I remember one time she got a couple sandwiches for a day's work. Do you think she ate it? No. She brought them home for her kids. Good mother. She told me the Russians, or Polish, she didn't know, shot at her. She went into a ditch, and she ducked low and kept running home to my hometown, to deliver the sandwiches.

My Duck and the Russian Soldier

There was a Russian officer on the beach as I was trying to hit a duck with a rock. I got one a couple of days earlier. But now I had this duck that was swimming away from me, away from the beach, and I still tried to hit it, but it got too far away. The Russian officer pulled out his sidearm, his pistol, and shot a few times, and actually, eventually, he hit it. The duck stopped paddling; he was done, dead. And I made enough fuss that that was my duck, and I wanted it because I needed it for food. I raised hell but that guy had no intention of taking it. He did it for me. So I waited 'til the waves, small waves, washed the duck to shore. I took it home and we plucked the feathers off of it and we had a meal. That was kind of important because food was hard to come by.

Bike Thieves

Me: I wanted to ask about a story with a bicycle and no tires?
Pop: That's right. We didn't have any tires, no tubes, nothing.
Me: But then you got a better bike from a Russian?
Pop: I stole it. The Russians stole all our bikes and they had them on the opposite side of Eiersberger See. And I went out there. Heinz asked me, 'Do you need a new bike?' I said, 'yeah.' He said,

'Go along the Eiersberger See and there's a house and they have all kinds of bikes leaning against the building.'

Me: And this is where the Russian soldiers were? In that house?

Pop: Yeah. They're the ones that stole the bikes.

Me: So, Heinz sent you to steal from the soldiers?

Pop: Yeah. He was clever. He wouldn't do it, but I did. So, I get there...

Me [interrupting]: Sure, he knew the right person to suggest it to.

Pop: Heinz was good in so many ways you know. Not like me. He was a good man. But you know, I went there, got the bike, but then there were Russians on the lake fishing. You know how they fished? With hand grenades. Pull the pin, throw the hand grenade into the lake, and the fish pop up. Bladder breaks I think. But what you do then, you also kill the young fish that are too small. But they could do what they wanted. They were on that lake in a boat, and I was with my bicycle, trying to get behind the reeds and bullets come by... pshhew... pshhew. When I was behind the reeds, I was ok. Then I got home to our house. I took the bicycle apart and put it in a pigeon loft so nobody could see it. Nobody could steal it again from me.

Death and Despair

There was this kid I went to school with named Jurgen. He used a *Panzerfaust*, an anti-tank weapon, to fire it. There was stuff lying around all over the place. He put the pipe against his stomach and squeezed the trigger. And that pipe got into his stomach, the backfire, opened up his belly. He was laying there with his guts out. I wished I hadn't seen it. That's something you don't forget. He was somebody I went to school with. He wasn't a close friend, but just the same, it was terrible to see. There was another guy, we used to call him *Zet Zwei Meter*. He was very tall. He killed himself, hung himself because he was afraid that when the Russians get there he would definitely be killed. I also know about a farmer and his wife. They were scared. They went into the Baltic and drowned.

Hitler Youth

Me: Pop, a story that had a big impact on me was the Hitler Youth capture the flag game.

Pop: I was in it, but I was not a Hitler youth, I was too young. The Hitler Youth and Jungvolk in our town played capture the flag with the group in the next town. We had to hide it. And everybody in our team knew where it was. So, when two big guys grabbed me by the arms...

Me [interrupting]: And you were the smallest...

Pop: Oh yeah.

Me: ...because you were the youngest.

Pop: Yeah. I was ten. You had to register for the Jungvolk at age 10. The other guys who grabbed me, they were probably 18, Hitler Youth. So I was taken over the cliff, one had one arm the other grabbed the other one, and then one asked me, 'Where is the flag?' I said, 'I don't know,' so he let go of my arm. I thought, uh-oh. Then the next guy asked me, 'Where is the flag?' I said, 'I'll show you, I'll show you.' So I went to that tree, where we had it way up in the tree, the javelin, and the flag, and they went up

there and got it. My team didn't like me very much for squealing.
Me: Well, your team wasn't that smart if they didn't guard their most vulnerable teammate. That is the obvious point of attack.
Pop: Right, that wasn't well-handled.
Me: No, and then when you walked back to town, they wouldn't let you walk with them, right?
Pop: They all walked together along the beach, and I had to go by myself back to Horst. It wasn't far, maybe a couple of miles.

Captured by the Russians

When my dad was captured by the Russians, they were marched east. I don't know where he would have ended up if he would have survived. Every day he saw someone drop, die, not enough food, or sick. He knew he had to get outta there. He escaped. He followed the coast at night and then during the day he would hide in the woods and sleep. I remember I was standing outside with a friend. He said, 'A strange man just went in your house, you should go see.' My mother called me into the bedroom and there was a man sitting there, skinny, dirty. My mom said, 'Do you know who this is?' 'No.' 'It's your father.' I went to him and gave him a big hug.

Paying Customers

You know, when my dad came back to Horst, he did cut hair for the Russian soldiers and the Polish soldiers. Both the Polish and Russians were in Horst. The Russian command post was right near us, where we lived. You know who paid? The Polish paid for their haircuts. The Russians never paid. And they didn't have to either.

Suspect Ham

Another time the German Navy was firing inland, against the Russians. They had their cannons along the beach. My Onkel said we got to get out of here. We walked inland, slept in barns, and then we came to a ham hanging in a—might have been a grain room for animal feed, don't know—but my Onkel said don't touch it, could be poisoned. We were hungry but we listened to my Onkel and we did not touch the ham. During that time, we slept in a barn. It was full of other refugees, escaping west. We couldn't all fit in. My mother got all of us five kids in the barn, but she slept with her legs outside the barn doors. In the morning there was snow on her legs.

Bullets were Flying

I think it was the Lithuanians who were fighting the Russians. They were shooting and bullets were flying by. My mother said, 'Don't you know what that sound is?' 'No.' So we went into this house for guests to that area and went into the furnace room to hide. The French guy who worked for my dad was there in the furnace place with us. We were looking through the ventilator fan and we saw the Russian soldiers coming. They called us outside and lined us up. Everyone thought that's it, they're gonna shoot us. The older people were more worried, I didn't really know what was going on. It was mostly women and children and old people there. Didn't happen. They didn't shoot us.

Around this time, we saw a dead soldier, a paratrooper, hanging in a tree. My mom started screaming and crying saying it was Paul, her husband, my father. My Onkel calmed her down, but it was hard to see her like that. It was not my father; he wasn't even a paratrooper.

Another memory I would like to forget is that I saw a Russian soldier raping a woman on the side of the road. I didn't really know exactly what was going on. I asked my friend, and he said I don't know, and we just hurried along.

Failed Escape

The Polish and the Russians were in town. There was a Polish command post and a Russian command post. We lived near the Russian command post. So what happened is, the older people, the adults, had a conference in private, talking about things. Of course, as kids you're always curious. What are they talking about? How come we can't listen in? It was important, as you will find out. One evening everybody was told to grab whatever they could and go to the Baltic where my Onkel Hans had a boat, a motorboat, good size, big enough to take every German out of the Russian section of my hometown. The men got on board and they loaded the boat properly. The women and children, I was one of the children, were hiding behind the winge. The winge was used to pull the boat out of the water and onto the sand. They used boards and rollers to pull the boat up. Anyhow, we were sitting behind the winge, and the women were talking. This Polish fellow, Lucien, he heard us, and he started running. Obviously, he would go to the Polish command post. I said, 'He heard us, we gotta get out of here!' We went down to the boat and told my dad and he said, 'Let's go.' We went back to our house. All our belongings were still in the boat. I said to my dad, 'Why don't we talk to the Russian sergeant so-and-so?' We went back later, the boat was empty, not a stitch of clothes left in it. The Polish had taken it all. Then my dad said to the Russian sergeant, 'My son said let's go and talk to the sergeant, he'll save our clothing.' And the sergeant said, I never forget this, 'Why didn't you listen to your son?' Well, my dad didn't have an answer. The sergeant went to the Polish command post and told them to return every piece of clothing. The people who put their clothing into the boat, they have nothing left to wear. That's all. Everything gotta go back. And we did get everything back.

Now, why did we try to get into that boat? They had plans to go across the Baltic to Sweden. To get away from the Russians. But we never got out there. My Onkel, he did a good job. He had enough gasoline for the motor and I'm sure it was calculated that we would get to Sweden. But it never happened. I don't know what would have happened if we'd gotten there. Maybe our lives would have been quite different. So that was the little story of getting to know the Russians and the Polish. We fought with the Polish kids, like boys do, wrestling, and I beat most of them, even so they were sometimes bigger than me. I was different. I was tough. The good old days.

You know, I think also, that Polish guy that heard the women talk behind the winge. He took off like a bullet to the Polish command post and they took all our clothes. That guy may have saved our life too. Because would we have made it? Did we have enough fuel to get to Sweden? That was the plan. The boat wasn't really meant for high seas but my Onkel, he was a good sailor. So I think, a normal sea, he would have gotten us there, if we had enough fuel. But who knows?

Escape West

One day my dad said we cannot stay here. There was no German schooling. We had to leave, and we had already made an attempt. This was in 1945. The Russians had a train going through Horst, to Trebto, and eventually to Hanover. Hanover was already in the west, that was not run over by the Russians. So one day everybody was marched down the street. Everybody who wanted to leave Horst Seebad went onto that cattle train. We didn't have the train where you have seats and all that. Oh-no-no, you are sitting on the ground, on the floor of these cattle cars. And then the train took off, so we moved from one town to another. Food was only what we brought with us, maybe a sandwich or loaf of bread, stuff like that. When we got to Hanover, which was a pretty large city, the train stopped in the train station and we opened the doors, slid them open, and we looked. There wasn't much left of Hanover, some church steeples, and chimneys. It was bombed out by the British and American air forces. But we pulled into the station, and we got out and we were fed by the Red Cross. They fed us food and it was so good! It was something we hadn't had in a long time! Then back on the train to Detum. Detum was a town, not far, it was at the end of this: it was Hanover, Braunschweig, Wolfenbüttel, and then Detum. And Detum was where we wanted to get off because my cousin Susan Eisensees had a farm there. By law, they had to take refugees into their house. She married a Nazi. She was in the BDM, the Hitler Youth for girls. We lived on that property. There were two East Prussian families, Krieg and I forgot the other one, but our family and the other Prussian family, they were living with my cousin in the farmhouse. This was a small village called Munchefarberg. There were a lot of Farbergs: Gross, Klein, and this was Munchefarberg, something to do with the monks. There was a monk castle, kind of, in the woods. And this one farmer was the biggest farmer in town. That's where the monks sometimes lived. I don't know the whole story about that, but the Eisensees were one of five farmers. So we stayed there.

Work in Munchefarberg

I did lots of different kinds of work in Munchefarberg. One thing I really didn't like to do. The farmers didn't want the rats and birds to eat the grain, so we could make a little money by bringing dead rats and birds to the farmers, a few *Pfenning*, pennies. What you had to do was rip the tail off the rats and rip the heads off the birds. If I would have had a tool, a little hatchet, it wouldn't have been so bad. I didn't like ripping the heads off with my bare hands. But you had to do it, so the farmers knew it was a new dead rat or bird. You couldn't just show up every day with the same dead rat and get paid twice.

I also did a lot of farm work, like picking beets. It was hard work and cold. Your hands got cold grabbing and pulling the beets out of the ground and throwing them into the bin. I was only ten years old and working with mostly women, but there were some men there too. Once I had a job where I had to load the greens into a hopper. I almost couldn't reach it, and it was so heavy. My father talked to the farmers and I got a different job. I could work really hard. My father was proud, but that one job was too much for a boy, so they gave me something else.

Leaving for Solingen

Now, my dad comes and says, this town only has a small school, a grade school, but nothing else. You can't go on and get a higher education. No way to learn a trade. He said we gotta get outta here. He contacted my Onkel Hans and his wife Tante Erna. My Onkel was my mother's brother. We went to Solingen and in Solingen, they took us in. My Tante Erna and Onkel Hans took us into their small apartment. My dad and I stayed there. I went to work at *Courtenbach und Rowe*, which was an umbrella factory. They made picnic furniture, outdoor furniture, and umbrellas as well. My dad worked there at the gate, to let people, trucks, and vehicles, in and out. I learned my trade as a plater. I worked in the plating department where all the umbrellas—before they were covered with cloth or whatever—all the parts were nickel plated. I got to know how to nickel plate pretty well, besides other plating experiences. We didn't plate gold, but I know how to do it because I learned the trade.

Spar und Bauverein

I wanted to get out of my Onkel Hans and Tante Erna's apartment. It was not a situation that you could maintain forever. We told them we are going to join the *Spar und Bauverein*, Savings and Building Association. That was an organization, if you become a member, you have first dibs on an apartment as soon as it becomes available. *Spar und Bauverein* built homes or apartment blocks for people. There were plenty of people coming   and going, from east to west, so we qualified. My dad looked around at two or three places and he decided on *Ritter Strasse*. *Ritter Strasse 47* was a *Spar und Bauverein* building. There was an East Prussian family on top, way on top. And just above us was the family Paul, last name. And we were on the bottom floor right side. On the left side was Dr. Zinn, a dentist. And another family, I forgot their name, but they were also refugees.

Machining

So it was kind of good. We qualified for that apartment and I got a job then. I didn't like plating anymore, because of the fumes, the acids, and all that. I quit that job, totally, never went back, except for plating in America for a short while. Anyway, I started to work at a machine company, *Forst*, in 1954. I worked there and did some work on broaches. Cutting the thread, like on the lathe...

(*I stopped transcribing Horst's recording at lathe. He goes on for approximately four minutes in detail about a broach job he did at Forst in 1954. This is a very Horst Ollmann thing to do. And a broach is not a piece of jewelry that you clip to your lapel. It is a machining thing. If you know, you know.*)

...So, let's get away from that, it really is technical and not so important. So that's what I did. Then I met my best friend, oldest friend, Gerhard Perschel. Gerhard lived maybe 10-15 minutes from Ritter Strasse 47. Gerhard worked on broaches as well. He was working on a surface grinder, a large surface grinder. The magnet was at least six feet or more, longer...

(*Horst starts talking about Gerhard's machining job at Forst in 1954. I stopped transcribing at longer. You're welcome, or apologies to all the machinists.*)

SLC | Solingen Leichtathletica Club

So, what happened is Gerhard and I became good friends. Gerhard joined Solingen Leichtathletica Club, where one of the most famous German long-distance runners was a member. His name was Herbert Schade. The city of Solingen built him a house, for one family, near Schauberger Platz, near the bridge that goes over to the city of Remscheid. I think it was Remscheid. Anyhow, that's where Herbert trained. And I was running on the soccer field behind Ritter Strasse 47. I liked to run, always did. I ran around that place and an older man living on Ritter Strasse came out of the back door and came over to me and said, 'You are running here quite a bit, why don't you join the SLC?' 'What's that?' 'Oh, you don't know?' 'No, I don't know.' I'm a young kid, maybe 18-19, I don't know. He said, 'Herbert Schade is a member of the SLC, Solingen Leichtathletica Club. Go over there to Schauberger Platz. You get to know Herbert and there are other people you can run with, training, go there.' I said, 'I will do that.' So I went over there; got to meet Herbert Schade. Herbert was running, warming up, on the grass, one lap after the other, not very fast; I was able to keep up with him. But I didn't know that wasn't full speed for him, that was just a warm-up run. Then when he was done with that, he would put on his spikes and do intervals. Run 400 meters fast, 400 meters slow, 400 meters fast, 400 meters slow, 800 meters fast, 800 meters slow. I tried to keep up with him then. Couldn't do it. That's why he was the fastest in Germany. He went in 1952 to Helsinki Finland, to the Olympics. And Herbert, and Mimoun, whatever his name was, and Chataway, an Englishman, and Emil Zatopek, from the Czech Republic, Czechoslovakia at that time, so they ran. This was the official 5000-meter final. Herbert was hanging back a bit and Zatopek was always up front, and Chataway was also in front of Herbert, and the Frenchman. Suddenly, Herbert was right behind this Englishman Chataway. Chataway stepped on a curb that separated the racetrack, the running track from the grass. Little cement wall no bigger than a couple of inches high, but he twisted his ankle and fell into the track. Herbert passed him and that was the last lap. Some people used to say after that, if Chataway wouldn't have fallen, Herbert would not have been the third, would not have gotten the Bronze Medal. But nobody could prove that. Herbert came in third. Herbert may have outrun Chataway, but we'll never know. Chataway got up but he could never catch up because there was less than a mile, less than a lap left, ¾ of a lap. So that was that. And it was so exciting to have a guy like Herbert in Solingen. We went on athletic events together to different towns. And we always watched Herbert, how he trained. We learned a lot from him. But never ever did anybody become that good, not in my team, my town, which was Solingen. Now I call Solingen my hometown.

The Color of a Dead Person: Repercussions

When I tried to emigrate to America, I had to go to Frankfurt to the consulate, where I had to fill out papers and have a physical. They took x-rays of me, and they found, in my lungs, spots, so I would not get my visa to come to America. I came home disappointed, and my dad said, 'You know Horst, what could have happened, when you were just a little baby that smoke in Oma Wilke's living room could have caused that damage.' Ah-ha, I said. My dad wrote a story, a short statement, and so did Dr. Johnson, who was our doctor.

Dr. Johnson said, 'There is nothing wrong with your lungs. You are a good runner. You belong to the SLC, Solingen Leichtathletica Club, and you have done really well running, setting records for different age groups. There's nothing wrong with you.' So I reapplied in Frankfurt. And that, Dr. Johnson's statement, and my dad's explanation of what had happened to me when I was a baby, they accepted all that and I was allowed to come to America. Gerhard, my good friend, and longest friend, we decided to go together, but because of my setback, a little bit, Gerhard left earlier. I said, 'Gerhard, when everything gets straightened out, I will follow you'. Gerhard got a letter from his Onkel, Herbert Thomas. Herbert Thomas said to Gerhard, 'Why don't you come to America? You've got three cousins here and you'll have a good time. You'll find work, and if you don't like it, you can always go back.' Gerhard said, 'Will you join me?' And I said, 'Yeah, I've already done it, I've gone through the process, as soon as I get the paperwork resolved or green card or whatever, I will come.' And I got over to America in 1959.

HORST TO HOLYOKE

My Oma and Opa took my father to Bremerhaven for his departure to America. Oma was sad; she worried that she might never see her son Horst again. Opa understood. He advised his son, 'Don't try to be somebody else. Be yourself.'

Horst picked the slowest ship he could find for his trip to America. He was 25 years old and wanted to savor the space between saying goodbye to his home and family and saying hello to a new adventure in America.

My father joined his best friend Gerhard Perschel in Holyoke, Massachusetts in 1959. In 1960, less than a year after arriving, he was drafted into the Army, 14th artillery, at Ft. Hood Texas. After basic training and eight weeks of engineering school, orders were cut. He ran to his barracks to find out where he was going. APO 696 didn't mean beans to Horst. He asked the sergeant who informed him it was Nuremberg, Germany. Horst said he replied, in his very best Elvis, "Thank you very much."

While stationed in Nuremberg Horst met Jutta, my mother. They fell in love and married. In 1962, after completing his military service, Horst and Jutta moved to Holyoke.

Part II:
HOLYOKE

Introduction

Explaining my father to you is an honor and a predicament. The best stories reflect on us terribly! And all the days and decades of love, admiration, and care are too boring to repeat. Horst is a storyteller. Whether storytelling is in my DNA, or a lifetime of listening has turned me into one, I am not surprised to be typing these words. Maybe Horst has been preparing me for this job since the day I was born. Maybe I have been participating in the longest job interview ever. Or maybe the stories and lessons from my father gave me the fortitude to just do whatever I please. I hope you laugh. Horst and I are ridiculous.

Horst Becomes a Papa

On January 19th, 1964, Horst became a father. Horst and Jutta welcomed their firstborn to the world, a beautiful and perfect baby girl, me. Horst called his sister Charlotte in Germany to share the news. After congratulations, her first question was boy or girl. Charlotte, or as I call her Tante Lotte, had welcomed five younger brothers, then a son, and a nephew to the world. Seven births, seven boys. She had no younger sisters, no daughter, or niece to spoil (more nieces followed but I was the first). Her second question, what day was she born? My father proudly shared the stellar alignment, 'On January 19th, same as you Charlotte.' I always looked to my Tante Lotte as an example of what a firstborn Ollmann girl should be and also how I was likely to age.

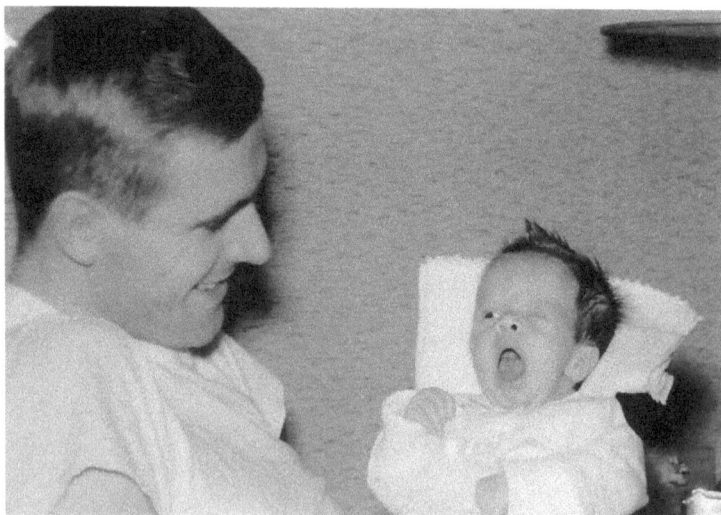

Baby Story

In our family, I am famous for speaking at a very young age. I like to talk. Of course, I don't remember any of this, but I know the stories by heart. This is one of my father's favorites. It was the summer of 1965, and my mother was making her first trip home to Germany since emigrating to the US in 1962. I was a year and a half old and my mother was pregnant with my brother. My father stayed stateside to work. We were away for a few weeks and Horst drove to New York's JFK airport to pick us up when we returned.

"You were being a little shy, you hadn't seen me for a few weeks. You were hiding behind your mother's leg, and you said, '*Mutti, mein Schnürsenkel ist offen.*' I couldn't believe it! Here was this little child speaking perfect German. And *Schnürsenkel* is not an easy word! That was amazing. I'll never forget it."

My Earliest Impressions of Horst

As a young girl, my father was a little intimidating. Horst is tall, 6 feet 3 ½ inches. In addition to his imposing height, he was strong and fit. Horst has been an athlete all his life: running, biking, golfing, hiking, sailing, and other assorted activities. He worked as a machinist and when he was home, he was usually working on some projects around the house. His hands were strong from constant use. This isn't only my girlhood recollection. Horst claims he was known for his strength: around the shop, they called him a "long ball hitter" because he could drive a golf ball further than the young guys half his age. Or so I have been told many times. Add a German accent and you might be able to imagine the intimidating part. All it took was a serious tone from my father and I jumped to attention. Not because I expected to be in trouble—because I tried very hard to never do anything wrong—but because I feared disappointing him.

Foraging

Horst likes to be active. Naturally, he loved to recreate his favorite childhood activities with his own children, both for his enjoyment and hoping to instill in us the same love and affection. We went along, as children must. Because he had such fond memories of berry picking with his father, we were also utilized as pickers. Sometimes it was a classic New England outing: we drove as a family to an orchard to pick bushels of apples and buy them. We picked and paid for strawberries and blueberries at local farms. Other times, we foraged. Once my father told me to pick dandelions from the lawn of the block across the street. Embarrassed, I went out and quickly filled a bag with yellow flowers. I never saw any other kids picking weeds from the lawn for dinner. Back at home, my father asked if it was a joke. Apparently, I was supposed to pick the dandelion greens for a salad. I was doubly embarrassed. First, for having to pick dinner weeds on our city street, and second for failing at my food gathering task. Both of my parents are knowledgeable foragers. During the war and later as refugees, sometimes the only food they had was what they found or caught. I understood how ill-prepared I was to throw rocks at ducks for dinner.

Trespassing for Blackberries

One day my dad got a lead from a guy at the shop about blackberry bushes on some vacant lot. He grabbed his accomplices, me and my brother Tom, and we drove country roads then pulled over onto the gravel in some forlorn location. We climbed over the "No Trespassing" sign hanging on a chain, our little green cartons in hand. I picked fast with one eye on the road, nervous that we would get in trouble. "Dad, it says 'No Trespassing', what if someone comes by? What should I say? Why are we trespassing?" Neither my father nor brother seemed concerned that anyone would interfere, or that we would be held accountable. I didn't know what the punishment was for trespassing. I suggested, "If someone comes, Tom and I can pretend we couldn't read the sign, because we're just kids, and I could pretend to help you with your English, so it looks like maybe we just didn't know that word. I bet they would let us go then. Just some dumb kids and an immigrant. I think that is how we should play it – you know, if somebody comes along." I'm not sure if this conversation was wholly in my head or if I voiced my concerns. Either way, same result, my worries were ignored. We picked berries until the containers were full. I learned a valuable lesson. You only need to pay attention to the signs and rules that make sense to you. And if you are feeling apprehensive, just do it anyway, if you trust the people you are with.

Seal-A-Meal

As my brother and I became teenagers, we didn't have to pick fruit and vegetables anymore. We had our own lives and paying gigs. Our mom bought produce at the supermarket, just like regular Americans. Sure, we had to plant gooseberry bushes in our yard because gooseberry jam was hard to come by at the time but picking in your own yard is different. One day, when I was a moody high schooler, my father asked if I wanted to go with him to pick wax beans. It was an otherworldly request and maybe I was feeling a little nostalgic, so I agreed to help. He had purchased a contraption called a Seal-A-Meal. Probably learned about it from one of the guys at the shop. He was eager to try it and knew a place where we could pick—and pay for, I made sure—wax beans. It was a sunny day and the picking was easy. At home, I started washing the beans as my father set up the Seal-A-Meal on the kitchen counter. I was focused on my task when I heard my father say, very, slowly, "Seal. A. Meal." I looked at him like he was stupid, "Dad, I think the heat seals the bag. I'm sure it will work without your magic incantation." He calmly explained that the bag needed to be in the sealer for a specific amount of time for an optimal seal: according to the instructions, the amount of time it takes to say 'Seal-A-Meal.' He was right, of course. Naturally, there was a logical reason that I was too ignorant to consider. But really, it was just fun to tease each other that way. We liked to highlight each other's stupidity!

House Arrest

Maybe you are feeling sorry for Horst. English is not his native language, and he never studied it in school. How awful to have such a stupid and obnoxious daughter. Just because my English *might* be better than his does not mean I am smarter. This is one of my favorite stories about my dad outsmarting me. Being stupid, naturally, I got caught the first time I skipped school. After being lectured by my mother, my father announced my punishment.

"Nicky, you are under house arrest for one week."

"D-a-a-d, in America they say grounded."

Then my father pronounced the word very slowly, exaggerating it in his mouth as if he were trying to shape the sounds, "G-r-o-u-n-d-e-d. Is that right? Nicky, you are g-r-o-u-n-d-e-d for two weeks."

I know my punishment was doubled, but I was so impressed with my father. Touché Horst, I deserved every bit of that.

The Woods

My father always liked to be out in nature. We spent time walking around the reservoirs, wandering the woods, or hiking the Mt. Tom range. We would observe the natural world as my father pointed out animal tracks, nests, and things of interest. At Whiting Reservoir, my father taught us about the speed of sound. There is a long iron railing by a little brick house. My brother and I stood at the brick house as my father walked a distance to the end of the railing. He had a rock, or piece of pipe in his hand; he told us to pay attention. We watched him strike the railing, and after a slight delay, we heard the impact. I wouldn't say that was very useful information, but what I loved was the wonder and awe of discovering and learning together.

Sometimes he would announce a challenge; he called it a test to see if we were "real men." Once we had to walk along a fallen tree caught in another tree's branches, well over our heads. He walked along below, ready to catch us if we fell. Mostly we just wandered aimlessly, exploring, and examining whatever caught our attention. One autumn we came across a young tree growing almost horizontally out of a small hill. It was me, Tom, and my best childhood friend and next-door neighbor, Lisa. We spent the day dragging big fallen branches to lean against the tree, creating a little fort underneath. We then wove smaller branches through the bigger ones and covered it all with leaves. It was our little makeshift lean-to. My father said he was sure an animal would make it a home for the winter. I couldn't believe it! I asked if we could come back and check on it. Sure enough, the following spring we found our lean-to. It was a little battered but unmistakably the one we'd constructed. My father pointed out animal droppings and bits of fur. I imagined a deer curled up in our cozy fort. Time in the woods is magical!

Speed & Battle

In the winter we played in the snow. Our father helped us build forts and tunnels and we went sledding and ice skating. Sometimes we drove to a neighboring town to an extra big sledding hill. It took about half an hour just to walk to the top. Tom and I went down in our plastic circle sleds, which was fun, but not as thrilling as going down on top of our father on top of an American Flyer, the classic steel runner sled. We hung on to our father, arms locked around his neck and feet trying to stay hooked to his legs; he steered the sled. We went so fast that it carried us further than anyone else, which really was a disadvantage because it was a long walk to the top again.

Do all kids love speed and flying? It seemed so. I remember the feeling of a dangerous activity. We lived in a two-family house. My dad's best friend Gerhard and his family lived below us. To me, he was Onkel Gerhard. Sometimes Horst and Gerhard would stand in the yard a good distance apart and toss a small child back and forth. I think it made my mother nervous, she could never watch, but I couldn't stop looking. I saw how they threw us through the air and caught us just under our arms, so gently, it was like they plucked us out of the sky. I couldn't wait for my turn. Flying through the air is exhilarating when you are certain you will be caught.

Most of our activities with Horst were outdoors, but one indoor game still makes us laugh. When my brother Tom and I were small, we engaged in an activity that we named "goofy games." Our father would get on all fours on the carpet and pretend to be a slow-moving ferocious animal. Tom and I used the aliases, Jack and Jill. Horst would growl and snap at us, then scoop one of us up with his paw-like hands. Jack, or Jill, tried to distract the beast and help free the captive. We climbed all over him. We battled the monster and survived, breathless and giddy.

Stories

I grew up listening to stories of WWII from both of my parents. It terrified me. I would ask my parents if we might have to escape someday, leave our home and belongings, and just head in a direction away. I would practice packing my little bag to see how many keepsakes I could carry. Even though they assured me that I would never be a refugee, I didn't believe they could actually assure it. It was just a thing parents say to calm a child. I mean, wouldn't my Omas and Opas have chosen something else if there had been an option? In general, our lives were calm and safe, but the war wove through our days in ways obvious and oblique.

I remember mindlessly jabbering about some toy I wanted when I heard, "When I was your age I wanted shoes, and food, I was always hungry." That'll shut you right up if you are a sensitive child. The first time I heard my father tell the story about the duck and the Russian soldier, I gasped, "Papa, why were you throwing rocks at ducks?" He looked at me in disbelief, like maybe his supposedly smart daughter had fallen on her head. In a slow exaggerated singsong, he said, "Nic-ky, we, were, starv-ing" as if I was truly stupid. Of course, I knew that, but it wasn't ever-present on my young girl's mind. It is not easy to be present for yourself and simultaneously vigilant about all who are suffering and have suffered before you. Sometimes I was just a kid watching TV and waiting for dinner. I wasn't even feeling gratitude, I expected these things: food, shelter, entertainment. Sometimes I could completely forget about starving refugees.

Food was political in our home. It was important not to waste food. It was imperative that we at least try a little bit of everything on offer. We were never to look down on any meal. If we were at a friend's house and offered food or drink, we knew to always say please and thank you and not to be greedy. But we were also snobby. We special ordered our bread and bought our cold cuts and other treats at Lisa's Intercontinental Foods—a shop owned by a German/Polish couple on High Street in Holyoke. Each week we got new cold cuts and added them to a Tupperware container. There was also a Tupperware container for cheese, which regularly included the Limburger my father loved and the rest of us loathed. On Saturday afternoons Tom and I would eye the fresh cuts, picking our favorites. Sometimes our father interrogated us, "Why do you always take the newest cold cuts? Who is supposed to eat the old cold cuts, me?" It seemed obvious to us. Yes. You. Because you always do. Sure, we will eat the old bologna, but not like this, mom fries it up for us when it gets old. Why shouldn't we eat what's fresh? Fresh is best. If there is nothing else, fine, but what's the point of choosing the old over the fresh? My brother and I just ate what we wanted and accepted that our father thought we were spoiled. I suppose spoiled is relative, like the old cold cuts.

When my father wanted to read us stories, he went to his cherished Wilhelm Busch book. The rhyming poems were fun to listen to, but the stories were foreboding. The most memorable was *Max und Moritz*, a folk tale about two mischievous young boys who enact mean pranks for no reason and then are ground up by the miller and eaten by ducks. It felt like a veiled threat, "Don't even think about filling my bed with June bugs. I will feed you to the ducks. *Verstehst du mich*? Do you understand me?" Of course, there were no explicit threats. My father read us those stories because he heard those stories as a boy and he thinks he turned out just fine!

Pay Attention

Sometimes I felt like my father understood me better than anyone else did. I don't know if he was more sensitive than he let on, or if maybe we were similar in ways that he recognized and understood, intuitively. I remember being young and anxious about some family outing. It wasn't a fun activity; it was more along the lines of an obligation. I was bombarding my dad with questions, 'Why couldn't we get a babysitter? Would there be other kids there? What am I supposed to do?' He squatted down to eye level and made a simple suggestion that dissolved my worries. He said, 'Tell you what, I have a job for you to do. I need you to pay attention to as many things as you can notice when we are there. On the ride home, you can tell me what you noticed, and I'll tell you what I noticed.' My mind was blown! I realized I could use the assignment to "pay attention" to distract myself when I felt anxious. Once I had a job to do—that I wanted to be good at—I didn't feel as nervous. I felt like a spy studying adult behavior while trying to make myself inconspicuous. This solution also provided an explanation should I need one. If an adult asked what I was doing, I could simply reply, 'Oh, just playing a game with my father.' I couldn't imagine an adult being curious enough to dig any deeper, so it was a truthful evasion. With a plan in place, I was ready to pay attention. I noticed so many things! I made a mental list to dazzle my father on the ride home: the wallpaper pattern, a run in a pair of pantyhose, a rosy-cheeked woman loudly laughing. I was hooked. Unofficial observer is a good occupation for the self-conscious. It helps to turn your perspective to the world around you instead of inward to your own insecurities.

Pizza Time

Most of our meals were cooked by my mother, so ordering a pizza was a rare treat. My dad and I always picked it up. We drove through what was called *The Flats*, crossed the bridge, and then headed down the other side of the river until we came to a bar. It was a small cozy place with a bar along one wall and a few tables and chairs against the other wall. My dad and I would sit at the bar. He would order our pizza and a beer for himself. I usually had ginger ale or Coke, and always a Slim Jim. It would take about 30 minutes or so for our pizza. Once I noticed a man walk in and pick up his pie. Excitedly I told my father, 'Dad, you know we could call and order our pizza over the telephone. We could be more efficient. We would just leave in time to pick it up when it's done.' I felt smart like I had noticed something that could improve our lives. My father asked, 'Don't you like sitting at the bar?' 'Oh no, I love it, I just thought we could be more efficient, I thought efficient was good.' My father responded, 'Efficient can be good, but I like our routine. I like sitting at the bar with you, and it seems like you like it too. Plus, we are here the minute the pizza comes out of the oven, so we bring it home to Mom and Tom as hot as possible. Having fun when you are doing things is also important.' I still love sitting down at a bar! I feel connected to all the bars I've sat at and all the bar patrons around the world.

Struck

A warning: My father taught me to be honest. He was always brutally honest with me. I could have left this story out, but sanitizing the truth is dishonest. People are flawed and they hurt each other. Children are vulnerable, and if they make it to adulthood, there are scars. As a boy, my father endured horrors I don't want to imagine. Trauma can be passed from generation to generation through stories and even genetically. Trauma is epidemic and hiding is not healing.

I'm not happy to share this story, but it is important. I learned a valuable lesson. I remember the first time my father hit me. I had no idea it was coming. We were sitting at our dining room table about to eat dinner. I sat with my back to the living room. My brother sat to my right, my father to the left, and my mother across the table. I asked my dad to pass the salt and he just looked at me. I wasn't sure if he was playing a joke or hadn't heard me, so I asked again, laughing a little in case he was being funny. Kids are notoriously bad at reading the room; it is a high-level skill that requires some maturity and experience. Maybe I should have sensed that he was not in a joking mood, but I wasn't thinking about him at all. Suddenly, a fork smashed down onto my Hamburger Helper, shattering the plate, and sending shards of Corelle Corningware, noodles, and ground beef across the table. I stared down in disbelief, then I was flying through the air and landed in the living room. A backhand from my father lifted me over the back of my seat and a few feet away onto the carpet. It happened so fast; I was in shock for a minute on the floor trying to piece together how I got there. I was ok. My father said I didn't say please when I asked for the salt. I hadn't, but I felt like I had probably accidentally done that before, without that reaction. I thought my father was wrong, his reaction was oversized. He'd lost control and I suspected/hoped he regretted it. It blew over.

At first, I really didn't know how to feel about the whole thing. Was my father a bad person? I love my father and I know he loves me. I behaved badly, or obliviously, but he behaved worse. Parents are human. Sometimes they mess up. We all mess up. It no longer felt useful to live with the naive idea that those who love you most will never hurt you. It's probably the people who love you most that possess the power to cause the most damage. I remembered the story of my father pushing his brother Heinz off the cliff in Horst Seebad. A deliberate impulsive act that could have resulted in a tragedy. My father regretted pushing his brother and was relieved when he didn't land on a giant boulder. I forgave my father because my Onkel Heinz forgave him, and in the end, it was good to know that should I need it, he would forgive me too. I felt a little bit of freedom. I didn't have to be perfect; I just had to do the best I could. And when I messed up, I owned it, learned, and moved on.

Job Stealer

I first heard this story when it was happening, as a young girl, but Horst and I have talked about it many times over the years. Horst left a machine shop in Holyoke to work at Berkshire Industries in Westfield. Early in his time there, the general manager talked to my father at his machine. He said, in essence, if you notice things that could be done better, or more efficiently, speak up, because they are always trying to learn and improve. My father noticed a grinding job that was being done on one machine that he thought he could do more quickly using his machine. He talked to the general manager and was told to give it a try, to see if it worked. It worked beautifully. He ground all the sides and could do many pieces simultaneously versus how they were being done. The general manager told Horst to go to the foreman and have the material moved to his machine. My father said it was better if that came from the general manager. He didn't think it was appropriate for him to go and tell the foreman what was going on. At some point after this, as my dad walked through the shop, one of the guys called out to him "job stealer". As a young girl, I hated to hear this story. I didn't think my father had done anything wrong. The guy whose work he took wasn't fired; he was just given a different job to work on. What my father said made sense to me. He said he was saving jobs because a shop that runs efficiently and does good work will develop a good reputation. A good reputation will lead to more work. Also, completing the job more quickly on his machine meant a better profit margin for the company because they were saving time. A smart company with a good reputation provides job security and stability for the employees. He worked at Berkshire Industries for 27 years, retiring at 65. Sometimes people are going to call you names at work. They may have different perspectives about how things should be done. I learned you need to be able to withstand the name-calling. There will always be name-calling.

Broken Finger

Every summer my dad's shop held an elaborate family shindig. My brother and I loved it. There were two soccer fields, a pavilion, games, horseshoes, pony rides, lots of other kids, and prizes. My favorite game was tossing a softball into a barrel. You got three tries, but if you didn't make it, you just had to go back to the end of the line and wait for another turn. Every kid participated because the prize was a silver dollar! That was a fancy prize in those days. They had a big sack of silver dollars, enough so that every child could win one. I still have my silver dollar from 1976 denoting the bicentennial. We spent the whole day roaming around and playing with our friends. Our mom checked on us periodically to make sure we were eating and not bothering anyone. Fun can't last forever though. When it started to get dark, my mother rounded up me and my brother for the long farewell on the way to our car. Every few feet we had to stop as my mother said goodbye and made plans with people along the way. I tuned it out and thought, couldn't you have done this before you dragged me away from my friends, but I also knew kids in tow signaled serious business and other mothers knew to let her get on her way. We found my father at a picnic table full of merrymakers. He downed his beer and joked and said goodbye as others laughed and joked along. Suddenly, there was some kind of kerfuffle, and we were fast walking to the car. I wasn't sure what happened because I wasn't paying attention, but as soon as the mood changed, I was back on the job. I was quiet in the back seat and looked out the window at the stars as if lost in a daydream, a disguise to create the illusion I wasn't eavesdropping. My mother was driving and asking questions. What I came to understand: my father was standing behind a seated coworker and started to massage his shoulders. His coworker grabbed his hands and started squeezing. My father squeezed back and then he heard a pop. He broke the man's pinky finger. I was astonished. I wondered what happened to adults who got a little tipsy at their work picnic and then broke a coworker's finger. Do they get fired? Reprimanded? Would we still be able to go to the picnic next year? I was fascinated to find out.

On Monday evening, after my father came home from work, I learned that nothing much happened. Broken Finger approached my father complaining about an insurance deductible and my father opened his wallet and handed him the $50 he was out. It sounded like Broken Finger was not well-liked at the shop. My dad said a few of the guys said he shoulda broke his neck. This was another valuable lesson: you can break your colleague's finger at a work-related function and not get in trouble, but you better be a good judge of the situation. This gray area was interesting. It seemed like you could go a little further than what might be advised if you knew what you were doing. I, naturally, had no idea what I was doing, but I tucked this lesson into my memory for future use. Years later when I asked my dad if he regretted it, he said he only regretted giving Broken Finger the $50. He wished he would have made him work for it, take him to small claims court. But then he admitted it was probably best to settle it quickly.

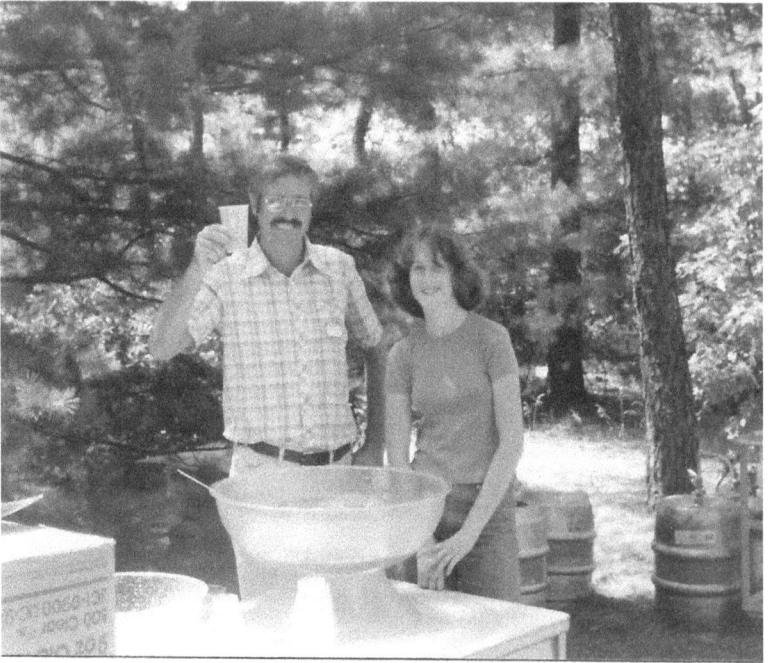

A**holes

A few years ago, I was talking to my mother-in-law while the TV played in the background. A young person was interviewed and asked what they learned from their mother and father. The interviewee responded politely with the virtues instilled by each of her parents. I quipped, "My father taught me how to be an asshole and my mother taught me how to endure torture." My mother-in-law laughed and said, that's pretty good Nicole, so I wrote it down. Later when I told my father, I asked if "being an asshole" was sort of an Ollmann trait. What do you call it when a man says "Heil Moscow" to Nazi soldiers or tells his neighbor that he should think of his kaka-covered rooster as a gold pheasant? I mean, you wouldn't call it friendly. You wouldn't call it nice.

My father often repeats with pride something I told him years ago. I said he taught me by example. My father demonstrated no desire to please everyone, so I felt like I could choose that option too. It is a powerful lesson for a young girl to learn. The lesson was not to act like an asshole and terrorize others. It was to stand up for what you think is right, even if people might call you an asshole. Don't care what other people think of you, be yourself. He never said any of this to me at the time, but it seemed like that's how he lived, and I liked it. My father always encouraged me to speak my mind and he had no problem challenging anything I said. He showed me how to be myself.

Ostracization

When I first heard my father's story about the Hitler Youth capture the flag game, I was angry. Why didn't the big kids on his team protect him? What would I do if I were hung over a cliff? I would give up the flag too. He wasn't participating because he chose to, he had to. When he turned ten years old, he had to sign up for the Jungvolk. I was especially mad that he was shunned and made to walk home alone. I didn't have the words, but I understood the message. I also learned something that was useful. My father expressed no anger or bitterness that he had to walk home alone. He understood why and accepted it. He was fine walking home alone. The group shunning didn't matter to him. I wanted to be like that. I understood that if I could build the courage to stand on my own, even if the whole group deserts me, I will have a much better chance of liking myself and ending up someplace I want to be.

Philosophy

My father is predisposed to antiauthoritarianism. He bristles when he is expected to follow rules because a so-called authority has issued them. He will follow rules, but not blindly. Horst wants to understand and decide for himself. He cultivated, or I inherited, the same aversion to authoritarianism. Like my husband and I always say, sometimes the best thing about a person can also be the most challenging thing about that person.

Horst will grouse when people nag him to drink more water. He will always mention that when he trained with Herbert Schade at the Solingen Leichtathletica Club, they never emphasized drinking water. That might very well be true. It is also true that knowledge has progressed over the decades. Horst believes in hydration; he's just opposed to the fraught hand-wringing that he must consume the exact fluid ounces prescribed by an authority. I believe in drinking water, but I can still see his point. The man is 87 years old. He must have figured out how to not die of dehydration. It's the nagging that diminishes the likelihood of compliance.

Sometimes that defiance or distrust is misguided. A knee-jerk reaction to something we don't understand. An inability to recognize the authority other people possess about what is right for them. I refer to this as Horst's hop-on-one-leg philosophy. My brother started playing basketball at the YMCA as a boy and played through high school and college. Either late high school or early college he announced that he was going to get a gym membership for the summer. It made sense to me. I figured he knew best since he was the one practicing and playing all the time. My dad grumbled. Gym membership was not as common in the early 1980s as it is today. He didn't know why Tom would spend money to go to a gym when he could just "hop on one leg up and down the driveway." I imagine I tried to communicate an eye roll to my brother, but we all just knew to ignore each other's uninformed or cranky comments. My brother knew what he wanted and to this day he has a gym membership. He has been working out at gyms for half a century and counting. Tom is an authority on what he wants and needs.

As a young person, I wanted my parents to not embarrass me with their immigrant ways and frugal behaviors. I also said uninformed and cranky things. In high school, in West Springfield, I returned home one weekend afternoon to see my dad sitting on a stool at the side of the road by our mailbox. He was shirtless, only wearing some short shorts and German sandals with socks. As I approached, I realized what he was doing. He had a small jar of paint and a thin paintbrush. He was hand-lettering our name on the mailbox. I said, "You know, they sell stickers with letters at the auto store. See…" I gestured to all our neighbor's mailboxes. Horst responded good-naturedly, "Well, I had some left-over paint, and I have a steady hand, and I think it looks pretty good. Don't you?" For the first time, I looked at his work. He'd drawn light chalk lines to contain the capital letters OLLMANN, and our house number, 24. I loved it. It was nicely uniform and did the job, but I was smitten with the handmade feel of it. My knee-jerk reaction was, 'Why is my father always being weird and embarrassing me?' But when I intentionally stopped to consider what he'd done, I saw the beauty and utility. Four decades later when I was using up left-over paint to hand-letter a sandwich board sign for my art business, I thought, dang I am my father's daughter.

Beer

After retiring, my father volunteered at Berkshire Brewing Company (BBC) in South Deerfield, Massachusetts. He loved working at the brewery. I think he mainly bottled beer, but he did whatever was needed. He has a lot of respect for Gary, the owner, and would tell me with pride when he helped to solve a problem. And he was paid in beer!

Once when I visited him in Belchertown, he mentioned that Berkshire Industries had inquired if he would do some machining work. He would be a contract employee and paid more than he made hourly when he worked there. Horst liked machining and he was good at it. I asked if he was going to do it. "Why would I?" he said, "I get paid in beer at BBC." I said, well, you would make plenty of money and could buy all the BBC beer you want and have extra. He explained again, "I retired from machining. Now I volunteer at the brewery and get paid in beer." Finally,

I understood; it was about freedom. Going back to Berkshire Industries would be about money. Volunteering at BBC was about beer, and freedom of choice. He chose it, he was appreciated, and he had fun. Success isn't about maximizing income above all else. Maybe success for him was about being able to say no to money and yes to free beer.

My Onkel Heinz visited Horst in Belchertown and, of course, Horst took him to Berkshire Brewing Company. Heinz is a photographer; he took a lot of pictures. He also met Gary, the owner. My Onkel didn't speak much English, but a shared love of beer can be communicated without language. Gary mentioned that they were planning a trip to Germany to visit different breweries. Heinz said they should visit him and they did! My father tells me they went to his apartment in Solingen, Am Kannenhof! This willingness to connect, even when language is an obstacle, is something that was instilled in me by both my parents.

Sailing

In the early 1980s, my dad bought a small sailboat, a Sunfish. You could haul it to the beach with a dolly and put it in the water from the shore. One sunny day, we drove to the Connecticut shore to take the boat out on the Long Island Sound. He made modifications to his set-up along the way, but on this day, we had to carry the boat across the sand, from the parking lot. As a teenage girl, I felt a little stupid having to carry a boat, sort of like having to pick weeds for dinner—it announced that we were new at this. I'm stubborn and stronger than you'd think, so I went along with it. Not at all surprisingly, a few strapping young men rushed over to help my father and relieve me of my ridiculous duty. Oh no, Horst wasn't having it. He told them I needed to know how to do things for myself, not wait for a guy to always help me. I didn't think I needed to know how to carry a boat, I think I was just participating in one of my father's tests to see if I was a "real man", like when we were little kids. Once we got out into the sound and were moving at a good clip, he showed me how to sail the boat. I was in charge when a gust surprised me and we started to tip, I let go of the sail just in time and we settled back onto the water. My sneakers went overboard during the near capsize. They were just beat-up old canvas sneakers, so I told my dad to forget about them. He insisted, so I had to maneuver as he tried to scoop my sneaks out of the sea. We got them both back and my father was so impressed with how I handled the little sailboat. I carried that boat, and I spent about half an hour trying to retrieve an old pair of shoes with holes in the soles. It felt like the funnest, dumbest, sailing story ever. Sailing sounds so fancy, but really, any idiot can do it if they want to. We did!

Talisman

My father has a talisman. An object he purchased as a young man to travel with him throughout his life. He chose it before coming to America and it accompanied him on the voyage. It is a small deer, standing about 6 inches tall. It is sewn out of fabric with a fuzzy nape. It is a realistic representation with delicate detailing. It's a stuffed animal, but not a child's toy. It is an object to be placed on a desk or shelf, a reminder. I always thought it was a little odd that my father chose this talisman. I couldn't picture a young man choosing a stuffed animal as a memento, especially a sweet little deer.

Once I glimpsed another deer. I perused a digital file through my cousin Susanne of my Onkel Rudi's *Wanderbuch*. My dad's younger brother Rudolf also emigrated to the US. Onkel Rudi, Tante Sylvia, Susi, Lisa, and Marky lived one street over from us when we were Nicky and Tommy, children. When Rudi was a young student, around 15 years old, he kept a notebook with drawings and notes from a school trip. In German it is called a *Wanderbuch*, a notebook to collect your observations while traveling. I immediately recognized the blue ink of many German correspondences. Onkel Rudi's penmanship was tidy; it was a joy to browse the digital file. One image is vivid in my memory. It is placed in the lower middle of the page with words written around it, compared to other designs and sketches in the margins. It was a deer sitting surrounded by greenery; a sweet, cozy illustration. My Onkel was quite a good artist. Maybe the image stayed with me because it reminded me of my father's talisman. When I was growing up, it didn't seem like men were allowed to show their tender, deer-loving selves. That little stuffed deer reminded me to notice the small and tender things that can be easily overlooked.

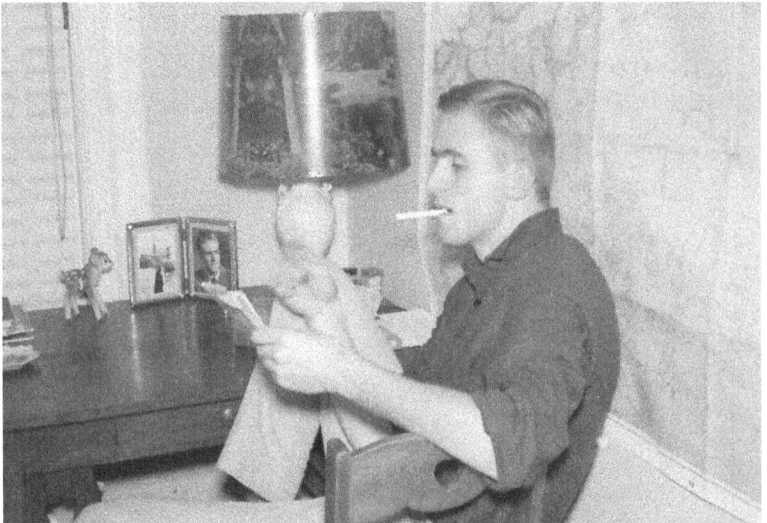

Inheritance

In the summer of 2021, I drove to Florida. My dad had been trying to get me to take his compound miter saw for years. Normally I would fly down to see him, but I had to arrange a road trip specifically for the saw. It is heavy! I was also going to pick up a painting of Horst, the seaside resort in Pomerania. When my father was a young man, his older brother Heinz approached him with an idea for their parent's upcoming wedding anniversary. Heinz knew an artist who painted outside at the castle nearby. He wanted to have the artist paint a picture from a postcard of Horst Seebad, a memento to remind his parents of where they had come from. Horst agreed that they would split the cost. Heinz was not as good with his money as Horst, but together they managed to commission the painting and pay the artist. Years later, Horst saw the painting again in his younger brother Wilhelm's home. Wilhelm was unfamiliar with the story but had saved the painting because it was a treasured piece in his parents' apartment. Wilhelm gave the painting to Horst and Horst has given it to me. It is of the lighthouse, cliff, and sea in Horst, now Niechorze, Poland. The lighthouse is a beacon to guide sailors. The pilings in the water were constructed to protect the land from the sea. A protected little seaside resort, like a big nest that keeps you safe when you are young and vulnerable and that you can always travel to in your heart and mind.

3' x 5' mat

A few years ago, when my husband and I were running the gallery we founded in Northampton, Massachusetts, I was listening to my father on the phone. I had just told him about something we had going on and he said, "For decades of my life I stood on a 3' x 5' mat. You, you have an adventure." And I thought, what is this idiot talking about? How on earth could he not see his life as an adventure? He lived through WWII. He emigrated to another country. He is bilingual. He helped raise his two children. He has run marathons. After he retired from the 3' x 5' mat in front of his machine, he prepared to ride his bicycle across America, from San Francisco to Portsmouth, NH. He told me that some guys at the shop cautioned him not to do it, saying he could get hurt or killed. He never listened to those people. He completed the trip. He also rode his bicycle from Florida to Massachusetts when he was 75. In between, he walked the Camino de Santiago pilgrimage in Spain. Again, people warned him not to go, that he might be killed by Basque separatists. He didn't think they knew anything about it, and he didn't listen to them. I have done none of these things. I am a typical monolingual American who has only lived in America. I've raised no children, I've hiked no pilgrimage, and I'm not very steady on a bicycle. My life is a great adventure. What I couldn't understand is how my father viewed his life as a 3' x 5' mat. I learned to create and love my adventurous life by paying attention to the people who inspired me. If my father sees my life as an adventure, he should know that his adventurous example is one of the beacons I look to for guidance.

Singing Songs

My father loves to sing. He has a nice voice. Even now at 87 years old, and with COPD, he will break into song regularly. There is a deep playlist in his mind, connecting music and experience. One of his all-time favorites is Harry Belafonte. Harry Belafonte deserves all the love; I just always thought it was funny that my introduction to Calypso music was by way of a German immigrant. In 2016, Horst and I visited his oldest friend Gerhard at his home in Easthampton. Sure enough, they sang *Day O!* together.

When I was a young girl, my dad made a trip to Germany. To say goodbye, he started singing *Leaving on a Jet Plane* to me. I cried and cried and cried. He felt bad, he hadn't meant to make me sad. I don't know how many more songs I will hear from my father but thinking of the silence makes me feel so lonesome I could die. So, I kiss him, and smile for him, and tell him how much I love him.

Prost

Cheers to you! We Germans say Prost! Horst and I would like to thank you for reading our stories.

We hope your stories are full of love, adventure, stupidity, grace, and beer – if that's your thing.

Epilogue

In the fall of 2000, my father slipped on the ice in his driveway sustaining a serious head injury. I was in Baltimore on a pre-decision trip to consider if I would relocate there for my job. Jim—at the time, ridiculously younger boyfriend, now husband of two decades—and I returned to our apartment in Springfield, Massachusetts to frantic messages on our answering machine. My father was in the emergency ICU at Baystate Medical Center; rush to the hospital as soon as you hear this. Baystate wasn't far from where we lived. Jim drove and I tried to prepare myself mentally for as many outcomes as I could imagine. I felt stunned and scared. I didn't know what I would learn once I got to the hospital. I contemplated my father dying, but it was hard to believe. Earlier that year he rode his bicycle across America. It didn't make sense to me that a fall in his driveway would kill him. In times like these—when you find yourself rushing to the hospital for a critically injured loved one—it's hard to know what to wish for.

Minutes after arriving at the hospital, I received what I needed, clear and compassionate information from someone I trust. Patricia Coffelt is an extraordinary nurse educator at Baystate Medical Center. She is also the daughter of Gerhard Perschel, my father's oldest friend, the one who invited him to try America. We lived together as children in a two-family home. We were Nicky and Patty then, aka Nick-Nack-Patty-Whack. Patty was a couple of years older than me. She was also a boss. Patty shepherded a pack of us younger children safely to and from Joseph Metcalf Elementary School for years. She organized activities and excursions. I followed Patty and trusted her. As soon as I saw her coming toward me at the hospital, I knew I was in good hands and that she would give it to me straight. Horst survived and slowly recovered, but he was changed.

Years later doctors said Horst had Alzheimer's. Then other doctors assured us he did not have Alzheimer's. The diagnosis now is frontotemporal dementia. Honestly, I don't care much what the doctors call it. He is just my dad, and he is still himself. I only need to meet him where he is now and love him. He knows who I am; I'm his princess.

I dedicated this book, *In memory of my father*. That's what this is, our memories, flawed, incomplete, anecdotal, clumsy, and beautiful. One day we will only be memories and after that forgotten. These days we just love each other the best we can. We know love is forever, no matter what changes.

Acknowledgments

I have received support for this project in many ways, from interest to encouragement, suggestions, advice, questions, book recommendations, and feedback. I am grateful to art history professor Craig Felton at the Smith College Art Department during the Spring Semester of 2016 for recommending *In the Unlikeliest of Places: How Nachman Libeskind Survived the Nazis, Gulags, and Soviet Communism* written by his daughter, Annette Libeskind Berkovits and for giving me *But You Did Not Come Back* by Marceline Loridan-Ivens, written about her father. In the Summer of 2016, I had the good fortune to receive the following recommendations from my brother's college roommate Steve Theriault: *German Boy: A Child in War* by Wolfgang W. E. Samuel and *A Woman in Berlin: Eight Weeks in the Conquered City: A Diary* by Marta Hillers. Many stories have filtered into how I thought about this project, but these books were influential because I read them when I was conceptualizing this story.

This book has taken shape with the generous support of early readers. Readers and feedback are invaluable gifts. I had the honor to receive feedback from author Julius Lester on a precursor zine I'd written called *Shot in the Head*. Julius's email is one of my most cherished correspondences, an excerpt can be found on the back cover.

Writer and fellow Elmwood girl Ann Marie Lucey provided feedback on early essays and zines including my first attempts at editing Horst's stories. Receiving encouragement and support from someone I admire is a mighty fuel. She helped quell my misgivings and early indecision.

Three friends read a draft of the manuscript and graced me with their wisdom and insight: Kaolin, John MacLeod, and my partner-spouse Jim Shea. As a fellow writer and cosmic traveler, Kaolin helped me to know what was important and true, think about the perception of certain language choices, and welcome the narrative that unfolded. Do-gooder hero and friend John MacLeod provided keen insight, important questions, and smart edits that improved readability. Jim Shea, well, he's just great and makes everything better. Jim was instrumental in designing the layout and cover and getting this artifact ready for print. For the record, all errors and inconsistencies are mine and mine alone. Through multiple edits, words and commas appeared, disappeared, and reappeared, moving, and shifting until I uploaded the file and called this project complete. Now *Horst to Holyoke* can have a life of its own in the world. Good riddance. Good luck. God bless. Be brave.

Images

Page 3 | Baltic Sea illustration. The pin is the location of Horst Seebad, in the State of Pomerania.

Horst in a Life is Good t-shirt raising a pint of beer and smiling at me on the rooftop deck at the Northampton Brewery in Northampton, MA, circa 2014.

Page 10 | Horst, a baby, and Oma Wilke. Written on the back of the photograph, "Horst-Seebad 1944 Horst Ursula *illegible* Oma Wilke." Horst at 9 years old.

Page 23 | Brothers Wilhelm, Horst, and Heinz circa 1945 in Horst Seebad. Horst at 10 years old.

Page 26 | Paul Ollmann in a black jacket at the head of the table playing cards with a group of men.

Page 38 | Horst with his mother Gertrude and father Paul at Ritter Strasse 47 circa 1960.

Page 39 | L to R back row: Gertrude, Paul, Heinz; middle row: Charlotte, Rudolf, Horst; in front: Wilhelm and Johannes circa 1960.

L to R back row: Johannes, Wilhelm, Horst; front row: Rudolf, Gertrude, Heinz circa 1970s.

Page 41 | Horst running on a track in an SLC shirt. Written on the back of the photograph, "400 m run in Düsseldorf in 54 sec 1955." Horst at age 20.

Page 44 | Paul Ollmann and his son Horst. Written on the back of the photograph, "Horst und Vater (Horst and father) *illegible* 1951." Horst at 16 years old.

Charlotte Stache (my Tante Lotte), Oma, and Horst in Solingen circa 1970s.

Page 45 | Horst with his brothers in Solingen circa the 1970s, L to R: Wilhelm, Johannes, Heinz, Horst, and Rudolf. I remember that coat. I imagined that my father bought it because he identified with the character played by Dennis Weaver in the tv police drama *McCloud*.

Horst in hat on a snowy Crosier Field in Holyoke, MA circa the 1960s. I like to think that Horst is paying homage to a favorite German artist/thinker Joseph Beuys (1921 – 1986).

Horst in tie circa the 1960s going for a Paul Newman look.

Page 51 | Nicky on her birthday typewriter circa 1970, Congress Avenue, Holyoke, MA.

Page 52 | Horst and daughter Nicole Suzanne Ollmann January 1964, Holyoke, MA.

Page 53 | Nicky 1965, late fall after we came back from Germany.

Page 55 | Nicky and Tommy circa 1976 with baskets of strawberries in the trunk of our first Audi.

Page 59 | Tommy, Nicky, and Lisa circa 1972 in the woods near Ashley Reservoir, Holyoke, MA.

Page 62 | Wilhelm Busch (1832 – 1908) illustration of *Max und Moritz* from Horst's book *Das Grosse Wilhelm Busch Album* printed in Germany 1959.

Page 70 | Horst and Nicole by a punchbowl and kegs at Berkshire Industries, Westfield, MA, circa 1976.

Page 75 | Horst with growler at Berkshire Brewing Company in South Deerfield, MA, 2002.

Page 78 | Horst with a cigarette at his desk in Holyoke, MA, circa 1959. His talisman, the small deer, stands on the desk.

Page 80 | Horst in Portsmouth, NH completing the Ride Across America in 2000 at 65.

Page 82 | Horst on vacation in the Catskills, NY enjoying a beer, 1997.

Page 83 | Photograph of the lighthouse in Niechorze, Poland, taken by Horst circa 2000s.

Back Cover | Photograph of the Baltic in Horst Seebad, taken by Heinz Ollmann

www.ingramcontent.com/pod-product-compliance
Lightning Source LLC
Chambersburg PA
CBHW040830300326
41914CB00080B/1984/J